CAPITALISM

www.heinemann.co.uk/library
Visit our website to find out more information about Heinemann Library books.

To order:
 Phone 44 (0) 1865 888066
 Send a fax to 44 (0) 1865 314091
Visit the Heinemann Bookshop at www.heinemann.co.uk/library to browse our catalogue and order online.

First published in Great Britain by Heinemann Library,
Halley Court, Jordan Hill, Oxford OX2 8EJ,
a division of Reed Educational and Professional Publishing Ltd.
Heinemann is a registered trademark of Reed Educational and Professional Publishing Ltd.

OXFORD MELBOURNE AUCKLAND
JOHANNESBURG BLANTYRE GABORONE
IBADAN PORTSMOUTH (NH) USA CHICAGO

Designed by AMR
Originated by Dot Gradations
Printed in Hong Kong by South China Printing

ISBN 0 431 12444 2 (hardback)   ISBN 0 431 12445 0 (paperback)
06 05 04 03 02   07 06 05 04 03
10 9 8 7 6 5 4 3 2 1   10 9 8 7 6 5 4 3 2 1

British Library Cataloguing in Publication Data

Downing, David
  Capitalism. – (Political & economic systems)
  1. Capitalism – Juvenile literature
  I. Title
  330.1'22

Acknowledgements
The publishers would like to thank the following for permission to reproduce photographs:
Bridgeman/Bristol Museum: p. 8; Corbis: p. 21; Corbis Sygma/Bob Daemmrich: p. 46; Corbis/Bettmann: pp. 10, 11, 23, 24, 33; Corbis/Charles O'Rear: p. 38; Corbis/David and Peter Turnley: p. 39; Corbis/Ecoscene: p. 43; Corbis/Eye Ubiquitous: p. 50; Corbis/Gianni Dagli Orti: p. 7; Corbis/Keren Su: p. 52; Corbis/Michael S. Yamashita: p. 49; Corbis/Philip de Bay: p. 13; Corbis/Tony Arruza: p. 44; Corbis/Wally McNamee: p. 30; Hulton Archive: pp. 18, 26, 29, 36, 41; Hulton Archive/Dorothea Lange: p. 21; Hulton Archive/Gustave Dore: p. 17; Hulton Archive/Lewis W. Hine: p. 16; Rex/Andy Hernandez: p. 34; Rex/Nick Cobbins: p. 5; Rex/Ray Tang: p. 54.

Cover photograph: Times Square, New York, USA, reproduced with permission of Pictures Colour Library.

Every effort has been made to contact copyright holders of any material reproduced in this book. Any omissions will be rectified in subsequent printings if notice is given to the publishers.

Our thanks to Christopher Gibb for his comments in the preparation of this book.

Contents

1 The spectre at the feast — 4

2 Where did capitalism come from? — 6

3 Building prosperity — 11

4 The dark side — 15

5 The crises of capitalism — 20

6 The politics of capitalism — 26

7 Capitalism's enemy, communism — 32

8 Capitalism and the poorer countries — 36

9 Capitalism and the environment — 41

10 Globalization — 46

11 So, what is capitalism? — 52

Timeline — 56

Further reading, sources and websites — 58

Key figures in the history of capitalism — 59

Glossary — 61

Index — 64

Any words appearing in the text in bold, **like this**, are explained in the glossary.

The spectre at the feast

It was the last day of November 1999, the new millennium only a month away. Ten years earlier, the power of world communism had collapsed, leaving the economic system known as capitalism in triumphant control of most of the globe. For over two centuries capitalism had dominated the economic life of an ever-increasing number of countries, piling up untold riches in the process. People in the countries of the developed West were roughly twenty times better off than their ancestors had been in the 1750s.

There was surely nothing to complain about. Had not capitalism delivered the goods and the good life better than anyone could have dared to expect? Yet on this day, in the American west coast city of Seattle, a rich city in the world's richest country, a huge protest was taking place. A protest against capitalism.

The protesters marched in their thousands, down streets lined with stores full of goods from all around the world, of every conceivable description. They marched in the shadows of huge modern skyscrapers, which stood like testaments to capitalism's growth and prosperity. This was Seattle, famous for the TV sitcom *Frasier* and rock bands like Nirvana and Pearl Jam, proof that capitalism encouraged freedom and creativity. If any place on earth had been truly blessed by capitalism, then surely this was it. So why were these men and women marching?

Their banners told a confused story. Many were protesting against the **World Trade Organization**, whose meeting in the city had triggered the protest. Some carried signs condemning a general lack of justice and fairness in the world. Others had more particular targets in mind – logging companies which were cutting down forests, junk food chains which seemed to be spreading like a virus around the world, industries which used animals to test the safety of their products. In the marchers' minds, all these issues were connected. As one Internet website advertising the event had put it, this was a global day of action, resistance and carnival against the global capitalist system.

No one doubted that capitalism had filled the shops with products and built the towering skyscrapers, but was it also responsible for the various problems and injustices which so angered the protesters? What exactly was capitalism? Where had it come from, and how had it changed during the centuries of its rise to global domination? Why were some of those who had reaped its rewards so keen to challenge it – or even to see it destroyed?

Police and protesters confront each other on the streets of Seattle, USA in November 1999. The protesters' sign points out the undemocratic nature of the World Trade Organization (WTO).

(2) Where did capitalism come from?

Capitalism is an economic system – a system deciding how goods and services are produced and traded. It has three key features: most property is owned by individuals; goods and services are exchanged in a competitive **free market** (one which is open to everyone); and **capital** (either money or other forms of wealth) is **invested** in businesses in order to make a **profit** – an increase in the wealth which was invested. Capitalism did not make a sudden appearance in world history, but developed through several centuries, its importance growing within certain key societies until it came to dominate utterly their economic life.

The seeds of capitalism

People have always owned things, markets for trading goods have existed almost as long, and capital goods of both types – **working capital** and **fixed capital** – could be found in any primitive farm. The seeds saved from one year's harvest were the farmer's working capital, the raw material out of which he would create the next year's harvest. The hoe he used to plant those seeds was the farmer's fixed capital, the thing he needed to make the best use of his working capital. However, he was not using this capital to make a profit, only to feed himself and his family.

By the 11th century there were an increasing number of merchants and traders using their fixed capital (a string of camels, perhaps) and working capital (a shipment of silk, maybe) to make a profit.

Attitudes towards wealth creation

Before the triumph of capitalism, attitudes towards wealth creation were very different. In the Christian Bible it was said that '...he who maketh haste [hurries] to be rich shall not be innocent' (Proverbs chapter 28, verse 20). Other religions had much the same distrust of those who sought wealth for its own sake. Such beliefs faded as capitalism became the dominant economic system, but as late as 1948 the Indian political and religious leader Mohandas Gandhi could say that someone who charged as much as he possibly could for goods was no better than a thief. Attitudes like his are rare in today's capitalist world, but have not completely disappeared.

For several more centuries, such people played only a small part in the overall economy. The odds were stacked against people like this becoming more important. Medieval organizations of craftsmen and traders, called guilds, decided what the prices and wages would be in their towns, and this made it impossible for individuals to compete with each other by selling their goods or labour more cheaply. There was also widespread religious prejudice against money-lending, which made it difficult for anyone to raise the capital needed to start or expand businesses. Those who did make profits tended to spend them on things like fine clothes and impressive houses, rather than using their money to make even more.

In this picture from a medieval illuminated manuscript, an official from the Guild of Wool Merchants is paying a weaver for his cloth. The Guild controlled the weavers' rates of pay.

Commercial capitalism

Slowly but surely, as trade increased and the use of money spread, the small pockets of capitalistic activity in northern and western Europe grew in number and importance. In the 15th and 16th centuries the vast expansion of trade which followed the opening up of routes to Asia and the newly discovered Americas introduced what became known as the age of commercial capitalism ('commerce' is another word for 'trade'). Most of the capital was still working capital – the goods filling the ships now criss-crossing the oceans – but there was also a large increase in those types of fixed capital which the new trade needed: things like ships and dock facilities.

During the same period, there was an increase in the making of cloth in private homes. Merchants would deliver raw wool (the working capital) to households where primitive machines (the fixed capital) would be used to turn it into cloth. Such arrangements were like a halfway house on the road to full capitalism. Two hundred years later, these part-time home workers would be working full-time in heavily supervised factories for a wage.

This painting shows Broad Quay in Bristol in 1720. Ports like Bristol grew prosperous as world trade expanded under capitalism.

A more favourable climate

As capitalism's importance to the economies of these
European countries grew, so people's attitudes towards
money and wealth creation also changed. Governments began
to encourage their merchants and traders, and to support
them actively against the merchants and traders of other
countries. Businessmen grew more popular as the older
ruling class – the land-owning **aristocracy** – grew less
popular. This was also the period of the European
Enlightenment, which placed a higher value on logical
thinking, a lower one on stability. The climate for capitalism
was suddenly looking fairer.

It was improved still further by the rise of **Protestantism**,
which triggered the European **Reformation** of the 16th
century. Protestants believed that nature was there to be
tamed, that hard work and saving were virtuous things to do,
and that wealth was a reward from God – all attitudes which
made it much easier for capitalism to flourish. It seems
unlikely that the simultaneous triumphs of capitalism and
Protestantism were a coincidence, but historians have
disagreed about the exact nature of the connection.

The Industrial Revolution

In the 18th century, capitalism's takeover was speeded
up still further by the series of inventions and technical
advances which historians came to call the **Industrial
Revolution**. The first industry to be transformed was
the British textile industry. The invention and spread
of new machines like Hargreaves' spinning-jenny and
Arkwright's water frame transformed what had been a
part-time domestic activity – typically, women working
at home – into a factory job.

9

The new ability to make cheap cloth meant enormous profits for those who owned the machines, and they invested these in new machines for making more cloth. Traditional cloth producers, both in Britain and elsewhere, struggled to compete, and by 1850 the UK's factories would be making half the world's cotton goods.

This machine is a replica of the spinning frame invented by Richard Arkwright in the 18th century. It was used to spin wool into yarn and was much quicker than previous methods.

The same was true in industry after industry. The fixed capital of the late 18th and early 19th centuries – mines, ironworks, potteries – spread across the landscape of Britain, Europe and North America, turning working capital into profits. These were reinvested in more capital, which made more profits, and so on. By the mid-19th century, capitalism was the dominant force in all these economies. Capitalism's growth machine was on the move.

③ Building prosperity

In the late 18th century, the Scottish **philosopher** and economist Adam Smith wrote a book called *An Inquiry into the Nature and Causes of the Wealth of Nations*. In this book he explained how capitalism worked and why he believed it worked in the interests of everyone, not just those fortunate enough to own **capital**. If certain conditions were met, he said, if most property was private and people were able to choose between competing buyers and sellers in a free market, then one person's pursuit of **profit** would end up benefiting not just himself but the whole community. What Smith called the 'invisible hand' of the market would work in everyone's interests.

Adam Smith (1723–90) was a Scottish economist and philosopher. Many people consider him to be the founder of modern economics.

How capitalism works

Why would one person's profit not be someone else's loss? According to Smith, it worked something like this. A businessman – businesswomen were almost unheard of – would borrow the money to buy the machines which he needed to set up a factory for making, say, woollen blankets.

The cost of making each blanket – what he had to pay out – would include **interest payments** on his loan, wages to his workers, rent or mortgage on his factory, energy costs, and expenditure (what he spent) on raw materials like wool and dyes. In order to make a profit he had to charge his customers more for his blankets than the amount it had cost him to make them.

So why would this businessman not charge twice the cost and make himself a huge profit? Adam Smith's answer was simple – he could not do so because he was competing in a **free market** with other blanket manufacturers. If he raised his prices too high, and tried to make too much profit, then people would buy blankets from his rivals, who were charging less. Competition kept prices down.

In order to compete, the businessman was involved in a relentless effort to keep his costs down. It was in his interests to make his blanket business more efficient by using better machines and fewer workers. If he did not, and his competitors did, then he would be unable to sell his own over-priced blankets.

This search for profit drove the whole machine forward. Businessmen in every industry struggled to undercut their competitors by finding new ways of making things, new things to make which people wanted, new markets at home and abroad to sell them in, anything at all to give them an advantage. The outcome was a whole new world of mass-produced, affordable products.

The golden age

During the first half of the 19th century, capitalism developed much as Smith had foretold it would. Most businesses were owned by the individuals or families who ran them, and not, as is usually the case today, by thousands of shareholders who play little part in day-to-day operations. Most businesses were also small by today's standards, and the fierce and open competition between them benefited the consumer.

The people of the time respected thrift, which encouraged investment, and they also admired those who were prepared to take the risk of trying something new, which encouraged innovation.

This was the golden age of capitalism. In 1851 the Great Exhibition was held in London to celebrate the progress which had been made. Thousands came to see the amazing machines which had transformed the way people lived. Even capitalism's enemies were stunned by the enormity of the changes. Three years earlier, in their *Communist Manifesto*, Karl Marx and Friedrich Engels had written that 'capitalism, during its rule of scarce [barely] one hundred years, has created more massive and more colossal productive forces [more machines for making goods] than have all preceding generations together'.

FOR INFORMATION ON KEY PEOPLE, SEE PAGES 59–60.

Visitors to the Great Exhibition marvel at the new machines on display, London 1851.

There was no slackening of the pace in the second half of the19th century. The rise of new industries based on oil and electricity, the development of automobiles and manned flight, all changed the face of the land and the way people lived their lives. By the time World War I broke out in August 1914, only small pockets of the old, slow-moving, pre-industrial world still existed in Europe and North America. In its place, the capitalist growth machine had built a prosperous world of cities and speeding machines, a world in which fast-growing economies went hand in hand with spreading education, widening **democracy** and flourishing culture.

Stock markets and shareholders

Businessmen often needed extra capital to make their businesses grow faster. At the same time there were many private investors with small amounts of capital who were interested in making a profit. So a system grew up in which businessmen sold the investors **shares** in their businesses, and paid them a share of whatever profits they eventually made. These shares were bought and sold in a market called a stock exchange. As individual ownership of businesses declined, and most came to be owned by thousands of shareholders, stock exchanges like those in London's City and on New York's Wall Street became vital centres of the capitalist economy.

4 The dark side

Capitalism's tremendous success was enjoyed by many people, particularly in Europe and North America. But by the end of the 19th century, doubts were beginning to grow. Many people had paid a terrible price for the wealth which had been created, and capitalism itself had moved far beyond the simplicity described by Adam Smith.

FOR INFORMATION ON KEY PEOPLE, SEE PAGES 59–60.

A different world

In the new industrial world, working conditions were usually unhealthy, the machinery often dangerous, the air full of poisons. For the first time in history, millions of people were working fixed hours under the constant supervision of others. Few of them had any say in what they were making, how quickly they worked, or what happened to the product after they had made it. They had become human cogs in a huge machine.

Some owners and managers tried to improve conditions for their workers, and to treat them like fellow human beings, but under capitalism the need for **profits** always had to come first. If a capitalist business needed to cut its costs in order to compete, then lowering wages or laying off workers was often the best way to reduce them. The workers were cut off from the countryside and the ability to feed themselves by growing vegetables or keeping animals. They were now completely dependent on their wages, and at the mercy of their employers.

Dark times

'It was a town of machinery and tall chimneys, out of which interminable serpents of smoke trailed themselves for ever and ever, and never got uncoiled. It had a black canal in it, and a river that ran purple with ill-smelling dye, and vast piles of building full of windows where there was a rattling and a trembling all day long, and where the piston of the steam-engine worked monotonously up and down like the head of an elephant in a state of melancholy madness.'

(UK writer Charles Dickens describing fictional Coketown in *Hard Times*, his novel about the horrors of the Industrial Revolution)

15

Of course, the more members of a family worked, the better the chance that someone would bring home some money. In the early years of capitalism, both women and children also worked long hours in terrible conditions because that was the only way they could find the means to live. The system thrived on their cheap labour, but a vast resentment also began to grow. Capitalism was producing wealth beyond the wildest dreams of earlier centuries, but it was ending up in far fewer pockets than seemed fair. Too many people were living lives blighted by insecurity, poverty and ill-health.

This photograph was taken in a cotton mill in Georgia, USA, early in the 20th century. These two young boys would have worked long hours for low pay.

The market grows less free

During the second half of the 19th century many working people came to support measures for reforming capitalism. They demanded improved conditions of work, a larger share of the profits, better legal rights. They argued that governments should give **benefits** to those who were unable to work, either because they were too old or because there were not enough jobs to go around.

They formed **trade unions** to press their demands on employers and **socialist** political parties to press their arguments on governments. In the period at the end of the 19th and beginning of the 20th centuries this pressure began to pay off. Old age pensions and **unemployment benefit** were both introduced in many of the richer countries.

These 19th-century workers' houses in London were crammed together under the smoking chimneys of the nearby factory.

This pressure from workers pushed wages higher than they would have gone in a truly free market. At the same time, their employers were finding that they could raise their prices higher than a free market would have allowed. During the second half of the 19th century, the size of businesses increased, leaving fewer and fewer in each sector of the market. As a result, there was less real competition. When only three blanket manufacturers were left in the market, it was relatively easy for their bosses to reach a secret agreement on what price they would all charge. There were attempts to prevent companies acting together in such a way – the American **anti-trust laws** of the 1890s, for example – but they were largely ineffective.

17

Factory work was often mind-numbingly boring. These women workers in a Liverpool factory in the 1920s are coating biscuits with coloured sugar.

Trade between nations was also taking place in an increasingly unfree market. The UK, as the capitalist world leader for most of the 19th century, was naturally keen to promote free trade between nations. The UK's products were cheaper and better, and would sell well abroad. For those nations struggling to catch up, however, the opposite was true. In order to protect their own infant industries while they grew, these nations adopted a protectionist policy, which not only stifled free trade but also helped to poison international relations.

Free trade and protectionism

In a free market the most efficient businesses prosper and the least efficient usually fail. In international terms, this might mean that country A's efficient steel industry would prosper and country B's inefficient one would fail, leaving steel consumers in country B to buy their steel from country A. The government of country A would be happy about this; its workers would be fully employed and its steel exports would be earning the country money. Where steel was concerned, country A would be all in favour of a free international market, or free trade.

The government of country B would not be happy. All its steel workers would be unemployed and it would be paying for foreign steel. It would probably prefer to protect its own steel industry by charging a fee, or **tariff**, on each ton of steel which country A tried to bring in. This would make country A's steel more expensive than it really was in country B, and so allow country B's industry to compete in its own market. The use of such tariffs to protect home industries is called protectionism.

By 1900 the free market envisaged by Adam Smith had all but disappeared, and capitalism was beginning to encounter serious problems. It was still showing an amazing ability to create wealth, but it was now also demonstrating a tendency to encourage serious conflicts, both within and between nations.

19

The crises of capitalism

World War I threw the world economy off balance. Some countries, such as the UK, France and Germany, had been exhausted by the financial cost of fighting the war, while others, such as the USA and Japan, had prospered. The decision by the victorious powers to make Germany pay **reparations** in punishment for starting the war made matters worse, and by the early 1920s the West European economies were in deep trouble. The leadership of the world economy had passed from the UK to the USA. The Americans firmly believed that capitalism was capable of sorting itself out without interference from the politicians.

The Great Depression

The Americans were wrong. Between 1925 and 1928 the developed economies did show signs of growth. However, there were already signs of a slowdown in the USA when the **Great Crash** on the US stock market in October 1929 triggered a collapse in the US economy. This led in turn to a shrinking of the whole world economy, which became known as the **Great Depression**. In the years that followed, thousands of companies around the world went bankrupt, millions of workers became unemployed, and trade collapsed. It seemed as if capitalism's famous growth machine had gone into reverse. Instead of success creating success, failure bred failure.

Capitalism no longer looked like a system that worked, and it even began to look like a system which was morally wrong. How, people asked, could one justify pouring away milk which hungry people needed, simply because they had no money to pay for it? Many critics pointed to the **communist** and **fascist** countries, which seemed – wrongly, as it later turned out – to be coping a great deal better with the Great Depression than capitalist countries were.

Post-war blues

'It is not intelligent. It is not beautiful. It is not just. It is not virtuous. And it doesn't deliver the goods.'

(English economist John Maynard Keynes describing international capitalism in the aftermath of World War I)

A queue of unemployed men in San Francisco, USA during the Great Depression.

Regulating capitalism

Faced with the Great Depression, the governments of the leading democratic countries – the USA, the UK, France and Germany – waited in vain for capitalism to sort itself out. It was only when this did not happen that they began listening to people who said that this would never happen, and that they, the governments, would have to do the sorting out.

The best known of these critics was the UK economist, John Maynard Keynes. He had long argued that the perfect capitalism of the free market described by Adam Smith no longer existed. Businesses and **trade unions** had been able to keep prices and wages high.

This had stopped the market from working as it should, and made it impossible for capitalism to regulate itself. Capitalism was like a boat with a broken rudder. It could still travel at speed, but it needed help steering a straight course.

FOR INFORMATION ON KEY PEOPLE, SEE PAGES 59–60.

Only governments could provide that help. If they spent money when the economy was doing badly – as it was in the Great Depression – then that would encourage growth.

21

The British economist John Maynard Keynes (1883–1946) was one of the first people to argue that capitalism needed regulating.

At other times, when the economy was doing too well, and threatening to grow too fast, governments could raise **taxes** and **interest rates** to slow growth down. In such ways capitalism could be made more predictable, more reliable.

The first government to test out Keynes's theory was the US administration headed from 1933 to 1945 by President Roosevelt. It worked. The spending programmes known as the New Deal kick-started the US economy back into motion and slowly but surely put the USA back to work. It was World War II which mopped up the last

The New Deal

The New Deal was the name given to the 1933–37 attempt by the Roosevelt Administration to overcome the Great Depression with a programme of government spending. Millions of unemployed men and women were paid by the government to do a variety of tasks – building new houses and dams, electrifying railroads, planting new forests, even picking up autumn leaves. The money they were paid was spent on goods, which helped other businesses get back on their feet. Slowly the economy began to grow again.

unemployment of the Great Depression, but the capitalist world as a whole had now adopted Keynes's ideas. Once the war was over, most governments, particularly in Europe, took care to manage and regulate their national economies. In Europe many large private businesses – like the railways in the UK – were taken into **public ownership** and run by the government. In both Europe and the USA , large increases in government spending – which were usually paid for by government borrowing – were used to stimulate the economy.

The result was a return to growth. Between 1950 and the early 1970s the regulated capitalist economies – including a newly lively West Germany and Japan – boomed, their industrial outputs increasing four-fold. New industries like plastics and electronics grew rapidly, keeping unemployment low. In many countries, governments used high tax **revenues** to pay for increasing health and **welfare benefits**. The growth machine was back on track, and this time it seemed to have a more caring side. Capitalism had become welfare capitalism, a system which not only produced wealth but also looked after all its people.

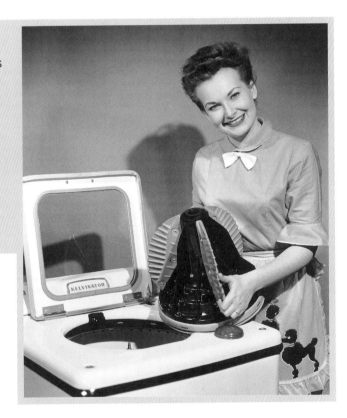

By the 1950s, the capitalist economies were booming and consumers had money to spend on new household goods, such as this washing machine.

A new crisis

The post-war boom lasted until the early 1970s, when the economies of the developed world found they were suffering from something Keynes had believed impossible – a combination of high **inflation** and high unemployment.

23

There was no obvious single cause for this state of affairs, and economists disagreed about how important the various causes were. Some singled out the rise in oil prices which followed an Arab–Israeli War in 1973. Some thought it was the effect on the world economy of US borrowing to pay for the Vietnam War (1963–75). Others pointed to the high level of government spending, which was needed to pay for the welfare benefits which so many now took for granted.

Whatever the cause, once again capitalism seemed to be failing. More and more people were losing their jobs and goods were becoming more expensive. The crisis was not as desperate as it had been in the 1930s, and this time around there were no obvious competitors to mount a challenge. Fascism was a disgraced memory, and it was becoming increasingly obvious that communism was unable to create the sort of highly developed economy which existed under capitalism.

During the 1970s, oil prices rose steeply and there were several scares about shortages in supplies. Service stations like this one in California, USA were jammed with cars as people tried to stock up on petrol.

Deregulating capitalism

Capitalism's answer to this crisis was to turn its back on
Keynes. The influential economists of the 1970s, such as
Milton Friedman and Friedrich von Hayek (both of whom
won the Nobel Prize for economics in that decade), argued
for a return to a purer, unregulated capitalism. They
wanted governments to create the conditions for pure
competition – by, for example, weakening the power of
unions to keep wages higher – and then step back.

Versions of these theories were put into practice by the
governments of Margaret Thatcher in the UK and Ronald
Reagan in the USA. They put many state-owned
companies back into private ownership (**privatization**),
introduced laws to weaken the unions, and tried to cut
government spending, particularly on welfare. Their
example was followed by many governments around the
world, although in continental Europe there was some
resistance to the reduction of welfare benefits. By 1990,
when communism suddenly collapsed in eastern Europe,
capitalism was more than triumphant – it had recovered
the dynamic image of the glory days of the 19th century.
The result, predictably, was two-fold. The last decade of
the 20th century was marked by rapid growth and an
increase in inequality, both within and between nations.

6 The politics of capitalism

Capitalism is a type of economic system. As we have seen, it has profound social consequences. It has changed patterns of working and greatly altered the overall distribution of wealth. But what political consequences has it had? How has capitalism changed the way countries are governed?

Liberalism

Adam Smith believed that the **free market** worked best when left to itself. Any form of government intervention was, he thought, a necessary evil at best. He accepted that government needed to provide those facilities which the market would not – things like schools for the poor, the armed forces, the legal system – but he insisted that its only other economic role was to remove any restrictions on the free working of the market. If the free market was like a river, then governments had to act like mechanical dredgers, making sure that the riverbed was clear of obstacles and that the water could flow.

This desire to liberalize, or free, the workings of the market was the driving power behind **liberalism**, the dominant political force of early 19th century capitalism. Liberals wanted to help capitalism overcome obstacles such as outdated restrictions on certain types of economic activity, or the continuing power of those – monarchs, the church, land-owning **aristocrats** – who felt threatened by the rise of the new capitalist class.

This painting shows a mob burning down a farm in Kent in protest against the British Corn Laws. These laws, which prevented a free market in grain, were eventually repealed (cancelled) in 1846.

In order to change such regulations, and to override the power of the traditional ruling classes, the new liberalizing capitalist class needed to promote and strengthen those **democratic** institutions which already existed in Europe and North America. In most cases they were only elected by a small, property-owning portion of the male population (no one else had the right to vote). These institutions could then be used to make life easier for capitalism.

Capitalism and slavery

The early 19th-century drive to abolish slavery, which was largely led by the new liberal middle class, was a good example of how and why capitalism encouraged the spread of liberty. No doubt many individual capitalists objected to slavery on moral grounds, but from Adam Smith's point of view the principle objection to slavery was that it interfered with the free working of the labour market. Capitalism needed free workers, who could move from place to place, changing jobs, if the free market was to operate efficiently.

Some of the liberal changes benefited everyone. The abolition of taxes on newspapers, for example, led to cheaper papers and a wider spread of information. This helped businessmen to make profitable decisions and increased the information available to ordinary citizen.

But other measures were of less benefit to the mass of the population. Giving money to the poor was discouraged, because it might encourage them not to work, and trade unions were outlawed because they increased the bargaining power of workers. The liberals of the time considered that both charity and collective bargaining interfered with the free working of the capitalist market.

Socialism

As the 19th century unfolded, capitalism's ability to create wealth was matched by its tendency to divide up the wealth unequally. Those with **capital** to **invest** always did much better than those who only had their labour to sell. Some help was given by governments to those on the bottom rungs of the economic ladder – the employment of children under the age of nine, for example, was banned in the UK by the Factory Act of 1833. However, resentment continued to grow, and in the second half of the century it found political expression in the growth of trade unions and **socialist** parties.

The central argument of these political groups was that capitalism, left to itself, caused too much misery to too many people. They agreed that capitalism was an efficient producer of wealth, but claimed that it was not able to make sure that everyone received a fair share. If capitalism itself could not do this, then governments had to. Socialists believed that governments had to intervene in the economy for the sake of the people as a whole.

There were several ways that governments could do this. They could pay old age pensions to people past working age and they could pay **unemployment benefits** to those who could not find work. They could tax the rich more heavily and use the money they got from this to make life more comfortable for the poor. They could even take unprofitable industries, such as the railways, into public ownership and use taxpayers' money to keep them afloat, thus safeguarding the jobs of those who worked in them. They could do some or all of these things, but each one of them amounted to intervention in the free working of the market.

The 20th century

The politics of capitalism in the 20th century revolved around the question: how much intervention should there be? A few extreme liberals still argued for the sort of minimal intervention favoured by Adam Smith, while 20th-century **communists** argued for maximum intervention, the ending of the free market and almost complete government control over all economic activity. Most political debate, though, has been between those on the moderate **right**, who favour a little intervention, and those on the moderate **left**, who favour rather more.

Those on the moderate right – most conservative opinion in Europe and a large portion of both major political parties in the USA – have usually argued that too much intervention threatens individual freedoms and makes capitalism less efficient. They claim that a free, efficient capitalism is in everyone's interests because it produces more wealth to share out, no matter how unfair the actual sharing out may be. Those on the moderate left – liberals in the USA, most social democrats and moderate socialists elsewhere – have argued that more government intervention can compensate for capitalism's natural tendency to promote inequality. It can help to create a fairer, more **democratic** society. Such an outcome, they claim, would be well worth any small losses in personal freedom or economic efficiency which might result.

A poster at Waterloo Station in London, announcing that Britain's railways had been taken into state ownership. This was one way in which a government could intervene in the economy to protect workers' jobs and public services.

29

Roughly speaking, the moderate left won this argument between the 1930s and the early 1970s. In both Europe and North America, government intervention in capitalist economies was far more widespread after the Great Depression than it had been before. But during the last quarter of the 20th century this situation was reversed. The moderate right took control and government intervention in most developed countries was systematically reduced.

There is no reason to suppose that this latest preference will last for ever. The very nature of capitalism – its ability to generate both wealth and unfairness – means that this political argument, between those who put wealth first and those who put fairness first, will continue as long as capitalism does.

FOR INFORMATION ON KEY PEOPLE, SEE PAGES 59–60.

During the 1980s, American President Ronald Reagan and British Prime Minister Margaret Thatcher both took steps to restrict the role of government in their countries' economies.

Capitalism and democracy

Some people have argued, and others have simply taken it for granted, that free market capitalism and democracy were made for each other. This is not true. Indeed, throughout capitalism's 19th-century golden age, the number of adults allowed to vote was strictly limited. **Universal suffrage** was only introduced in the richer countries in the 20th century, and it has still not been introduced in some countries – Saudi Arabia is one example – which play an important role in the world capitalist system.

Certain features of capitalism have favoured democracy, especially in the developed countries. For capitalism to work, individuals must have economic freedom, and political freedom seems like the natural next step. However, other aspects of capitalism have worked against democracy, particularly its tendency to create inequality. The political equality of one person–one vote means a lot less when some people have so much more economic power than others.

Capitalism and freedom

Capitalism and freedom are often bracketed together, as if they are virtually the same thing. This is only partly true. Capitalism needs a free market – that is, one in which governments try not to interfere in the buying and selling of goods and services. It also relies on a spirit of free enterprise, on individual ambition and initiative. It requires what **philosophers** have called the 'freedoms to' – such as to trade, or speak their mind – those freedoms which allow people to do what they individually wish to do within agreed rules of law.

Capitalism does not, however, need the full range of political freedoms which are generally enjoyed in early 21st-century Europe and North America in order to operate. It has worked perfectly well in a variety of political environments – **colonial rule**, civil and military **dictatorship**, even communist dictatorships like present-day China – where political freedoms have been severely limited. Capitalism has also often failed to make room for what philosophers call the 'freedoms from', like freedom from hunger, unemployment, insecurity and fear.

Capitalism's enemy, communism

Capitalism faced two great challenges in the 20th century. The first of these came from within. It involved reforming and regulating itself to the point where it became acceptable to a large majority of the population. The second, the challenge of **communism**, came from outside. This second challenge was political, economic and, at times, even military.

Communism comes to power

Communism was a response to capitalism's failure in certain parts of the world. In Russia, where the first communist revolution took place in October 1917, capitalism's dark side – the appalling conditions of work and the growing inequalities – had been very obvious. Few people had benefited from capitalism's ability to create wealth. Much of the capital invested in Russia before World War I had come from other countries, and few of the **profits** were seen by ordinary Russians. When Lenin's victorious Communist Party announced that they intended to abolish capitalism, and create a kind of **socialism** in its place, many Russians rejoiced.

Similar chains of events later took place in China and Cuba. Before their revolutions – in 1949 and 1959 respectively – both countries experienced many of capitalism's negative points but few of its plus points, and both peoples were willing, at least in the beginning, to try and create something different.

Abolishing capitalism

The Russian communists abolished capitalism. The private ownership of most property was brought to an end, leaving no basis for a competitive free market. All economic decisions – what to produce, where and how to produce it – were now taken by the 'visible hand' of government rather than what Adam Smith called the 'invisible hand' of the free market. The government planners decided to invest in a new steel mill or a new dam because they thought the country needed such things, not because they expected to make a profit out of them.

FOR INFORMATION ON KEY PEOPLE, SEE PAGES 59–60.

This, the communists claimed, was both more rational –
it meant that only what was really needed got produced –
and fairer. There were no capitalists at the top enjoying
huge profits, no workers at the bottom slaving away for
others' gain.

There was some truth in this, but only some. It turned out
that economic planning only worked well in the early
stages of industrialization; once the economy grew more
complicated, the 'visible hand' of government direction
proved much more clumsy and inefficient than the
'invisible hand' of the market. It also turned out that,
profits or no profits, those who ran the system still
managed to enjoy an unfair share of what was produced.
Communism was no fairer than capitalism.

The message on this
propaganda poster from
the Russian Revolution is:
'You still haven't joined
the Co-operative – sign
up immediately!'

Finally, and perhaps most importantly of all, the lack of economic freedom went hand in hand with a lack of political freedom. Creativity was stifled, innovation discouraged, individual ambition and enthusiasm dulled. Communism lacked the very things which had turned capitalism into a growth machine.

Lenin on capitalism

'Capitalists are no more capable of self-sacrifice than a man is capable of lifting himself up by his own bootstraps.'

(Russian communist leader Vladimir Lenin, stating his belief that, under capitalism, the rich did not want to help the poor and the poor were unable to help themselves.)

Cold War

Communism's failings took a long time to become apparent. In the 1930s, when the leading capitalist countries were dragging along the bottom of the Great Depression, communist Russia seemed to be forging ahead with its ambitious **five-year plans**. The level of suffering in the West was well known, the much greater level of suffering in Russia hardly known at all. Russian military success in World War II and the amazing economic recovery which followed only heightened the communist reputation.

During the final years of the communist Soviet Union, there were shortages of many goods. People often had to queue for hours just to buy food.

By 1950, however, the capitalist world had also recovered economically, and through the first twenty years of the **Cold War** (1948–68) each of the two systems tried to prove that it was more efficient than the other. Capitalism and communism also competed for influence in the developing countries of Asia, Africa and Latin America, where the capitalist world was at a definite disadvantage. For one thing, the capitalist countries – either as colonial powers or simple economic bullies – were considered responsible for the poverty which existed throughout the developing world. For another, communism did seem good at providing the sort of basic economic development which many of the poorer countries so desperately needed. It had worked for Russia and China, so why not for other undeveloped countries?

Eventually, however, the failure of the communist countries to produce the wide range of goods which their own peoples wanted, and which the advanced capitalist countries took for granted, resulted in the collapse of European communism and an end, in all but name, to communism in east Asia. By 1991, capitalism's triumph over its enemy was virtually complete.

The only sour note was the continuing poverty of many developing-world countries. It was this that had produced so much hostility towards capitalism in the developing world, and so much popularity for communism.

⑧ Capitalism and the poorer countries

The enormous wealth which capitalism generated through the 19th and 20th centuries was not spread evenly across the globe. Some countries were much richer than others, and inside all countries some people were much richer than others. As the 20th century drew to a close, these gaps were growing wider rather than narrower. Around a quarter of the world's people – most of them living in the world's poorest countries – had an income of less than £250 ($370) a year. For these people, capitalism was obviously not working very well.

Colonialism and after

Some people blamed this situation on **colonialism**, the rule of economically undeveloped countries by economically advanced countries. They claimed that European powers like the UK and France, which had ruled large parts of the world for several centuries, had held back those countries which they occupied.

This painting shows British ships lining the quays at the port of Calcutta in India during the days of the British Empire.

Rather than give or sell modern technology to these countries, and let them create their own industrial revolution, these colonial powers had used such countries as sources of raw materials and markets for their own industrial products. The UK, for example, had arranged taxes and **tariffs** in such a way that their own cotton manufacturers were able to undercut Indian cotton manufacturers even in India.

However, supporters of colonialism have pointed out that the capitalist powers also improved the basic facilities of the countries they occupied. They left them with better roads, railways and docks, and better-organized systems of law and administration.

Most direct colonial rule came to an end during the second half of the 20th century, but those most critical of the rich countries' behaviour in what became known as the 'third' (or developing) world argue that little really changed. Countries were given political independence, but they were still economically dependent on the richer countries. The World Bank and International Monetary Fund were supposed to provide help, but they were effectively controlled by the USA and the old colonial powers.

Overseeing the international economy

There are three major international economic organizations. The International Bank for Reconstruction and Development (generally known as the World Bank) and the International Monetary Fund (IMF) were both formed in 1945 with the aim of encouraging world economic development. Both have loaned large amounts of money to the developing countries, much of which they have been unable to repay. In the late 1990s, a worldwide campaign was launched to cancel many of the outstanding debts.

The **World Trade Organization (WTO)** was founded in 1995 as the successor to the General Agreement on Tariffs and Trade (GATT). Its main task is to regulate trade and, where possible, take away barriers to free trade. Since free trade tends to benefit the richer, more efficient producing countries, the WTO has also been subject to a campaign of protest.

According to capitalism's critics, people and businesses in the richer countries held on to most of the economic power. They decided where to invest their capital in new businesses and jobs. The poorer countries, rather like ordinary UK or US workers in the early 19th century, had to accept whatever they were offered. They had little bargaining power of their own.

Capitalism's supporters had a more positive view of its record in the developing world. They pointed to the success of what were called the '**Asian Tigers**' – countries like South Korea, Taiwan, Singapore and Malaysia – which had managed to lift themselves out of poverty by stressing education and hard work, and by keeping wages low. These countries had successfully competed with the rich nations by doing exactly what Adam Smith would have recommended. They had made products the richer nations wanted, more cheaply and efficiently than the rich nations could do it themselves.

This assembly plant in Durban, South Africa is owned by the Japanese company, Toyota. Multinational corporations like Toyota provide jobs for people in many of the world's poorer countries.

Opting out

The most important change to affect the international economy over the last quarter century has been the growing importance of **multinational corporations**. These businesses, which conduct operations all around the world, often have higher incomes and expenditure than national governments. Their supporters have claimed that they bring new technology, new management methods and new jobs to the poorer countries, and should therefore be welcomed. Their critics argued that the jobs are few, that major decisions are all taken at corporate headquarters in the rich countries, and that most of the profits are sent home to the richer countries. These critics have claimed that the multinational corporations, far from developing the poorer countries, are using them as a source of cheap labour.

In order to protect themselves from the overwhelming power of foreign economic interests, some of the poorer countries have tried to opt out of the world capitalist system. In the early 1960s, for example, Cuba joined the communist world when its revolutionary leaders realized that staying in the capitalist system would mean domination by its neighbour the USA. In Tanzania, President Julius Nyerere tried to introduce a form of African socialism in semi-isolation from the capitalist world, and other developing-world countries have made occasional attempts to go it alone.

There have been some successes – Cuba's system of health care, for example, is considered by many the best in Latin America – but generally speaking these and other attempts by small countries to step outside the capitalist system have been a failure. Capitalism has been too powerful for them in almost every respect. Its economic success has been impossible to ignore, its economic power – and sometimes its military power – impossible to resist.

These women and children in Egypt survive by rummaging through a dump in search of food and things to sell. Critics of multinational corporations claim that they often do not bring wealth to the poorer countries where their factories are based.

Extending welfare capitalism?

Over the last hundred years the whole world has learned what Europe and North America learned in the 19th century, that capitalism creates both wealth and inequality. The European and North American answer was to regulate and reform capitalism to the point where it offered something even to those at the bottom of the economic ladder. If the widening gap between rich and poor countries is to be narrowed, it seems likely that something similar must be introduced at the international level. How this can be achieved, when there is no prospect of meaningful international government, is one of the most important questions facing people and politicians in the 21st century.

⑨ Capitalism and the environment

If capitalism did manage to raise the economic level of the world's poorer countries to that enjoyed today by the richer countries, it would, unfortunately, find itself with another problem. Experts have estimated that this level of world economic growth would need a five-fold increase in energy consumption, at a time when current levels are already creating major problems for the environment.

Dark beginnings

As early as 1804 the British writer William Blake, in his famous poem which became the text for the hymn 'Jerusalem', contrasted the dark satanic (hell-like) mills of the **Industrial Revolution** with the green and pleasant land which they were replacing, and as the century unfolded things only changed for the worse. Each year thousands of new factories in western Europe and North America coughed coal smoke and unhealthy gases into the air, darkening the daytime sky over rapidly growing towns.

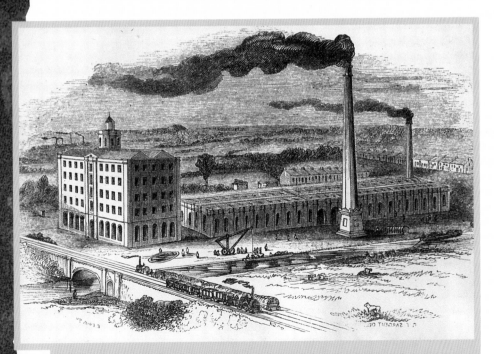

This painting from 1840 shows a newly built metalworks in Somerset. The writer William Blake was critical of the way that factories like this one were spoiling the English countryside.

Few governments made any attempts to limit either this poisoning of the atmosphere, or the poisoning of the rivers with industrial waste. For well over a century, capitalist industry was allowed to take its profits without cleaning up after itself.

Things began to change around the middle of the 20th century. The areas affected by industrial pollution had slowly grown, and now included large parts of the most developed countries. The UK capital London, for example, experienced serious smogs (industrial fogs) in the early 1950s. One of them is said to have killed several hundred people. Both in London and elsewhere a serious effort was made to clean up industry. This was made easier by the fact that coal-fired industries were, in many cases, already giving way to alternatives which caused less pollution.

Limits to growth?

The next major environmental crisis came in the mid-1970s. Experts claimed that the world s population was increasing too fast, and that at current rates the world would soon exhaust its stocks of raw materials like oil and minerals that could not be replaced. They argued that there was a limit to growth, and that the world would need a replacement for capitalism s growth machine, which was unable to stand still. By the end of the 20th century, though, the expected shortages had not come to pass. New experts claimed that they never would, that capitalism s restless genius would always find new alternatives, new ways of doing things when old ones no longer worked.

There were still many doubters, however. They pointed to events like the continuing destructions of the rainforests, and stressed the risks humanity was running by using up its resources at such a rate.

This area of Malaysian rainforest has been cleared of trees to make way for agriculture. Environmental experts are worried that cutting down rainforests may be contributing to global warming.

In the meantime, other dangers of headlong growth were becoming apparent. The most important of these was **global warming**. According to scientists, a steady rise in the amount of industrial emissions pumped into the atmosphere was raising the global temperature, with serious consequences for sea levels and local climates. Once again many voices were heard insisting that capitalism's growth machine had to be slowed or even halted in its tracks.

Capitalism's problem?

It could be argued that industrialism, and not capitalism, was responsible for these problems – the **communist** world's environmental record had been just as bad, if not worse. By the end of the 20th century, though, capitalism was responsible for almost all of the world's industrial growth, and almost all of the environmental problems such growth created. So was capitalism an efficient system for putting things right?

43

Adam Smith's argument – that individuals pursuing their own individual interest will end up benefiting everyone – clearly does not work where the environment is concerned. Factory owners who cut costs by dropping poisonous waste in the river are both helping themselves and harming the community. They are also encouraging their competitors to do the same, because that is the only way they can compete. The only way around this is for governments to pass laws against such behaviour, and then enforce the laws.

This can work within countries, but in the world at large it is much harder either to agree or enforce such regulations. The USA decided in 2001 to withdraw from the 1997 Kyoto Agreement on limiting the emissions which lead to global warming. This was an indication of how hard it may be, in a competitive, capitalist world, to persuade nations to set aside their own self-interest in the interests of the wider world.

Too many cars – a traffic jam in Boston, USA contributes to the global warming problem.

44

Capitalism's solutions?

There has been a huge growth in the sale of so-called green products – things like enzyme-free washing powders, long-life light bulbs and electric cars – which are either environment-friendly or save on scarce resources. Governments have encouraged recycling of waste products, and there has been a steep rise in the practice of charging both businesses and individuals for the damage they do to the environment. Factory owners, who once simply dumped their waste in a river and thought no more about it, now have to pay for safe disposal or face heavy fines.

Road pricing

Road pricing is a good example of how, under capitalism, polluters can be made to pay for the pollution they cause. If car owners are charged for using city streets, they will then use their cars less, which will lower the level of exhaust emissions. When they do choose to pay the charges and use their cars, the money collected can be used to improve public transport systems. Once public transport is improved, more people will choose to use it, and this will lessen pollution still more. And in the meantime, the high cost of using cars which pollute will have created a new and growing market for cars that do not.

Measures like these include the cost of preserving the environment in the overall cost of goods and services. Supporters of capitalism believe that this will be enough to solve the world's environmental problems. There is no need, they say, for serious reforms or to abandon capitalism. Others believe that this approach, if it works at all, will work far too slowly. They believe that the environmental crisis facing the capitalist world of the 21st century is every bit as serious as that which faced capitalism in the 1930s. It will only be overcome by government intervention on a similar scale.

⑩ Globalization

In the final decade of the 20th century, capitalism took over almost the whole international economy. The end of communism in Europe and the parallel opening up of **communist** China to capitalist enterprise were two reasons for this process of globalization, but they were not the only ones. The advances in telecommunications and computing, which meant the whole world could be reached, and the growth of **multinational corporations** which make use of this were even more important.

In the 1980s and 1990s many restrictions on international trade were removed, and the multinational corporations were able to start moving their capital around the world in search of the best deals. Not surprisingly, they often chose to set up their operations in poorer countries like Mexico or Indonesia, where cheaper labour (workers who cost less) would bring down the cost of production. It also often made sense for them to get local firms to do the actual manufacturing. That way, the corporation would not have to pay the local workers unemployment or health benefits.

American workers in Austin, Texas demonstrate against the North American Free Trade Association in November 1993. Many are afraid that companies will move their operations to Mexico, where wages are lower.

Consequences for the richer countries

Capitalism's globalization has had important consequences for all countries, from the richest to the poorest. The rich countries certainly grew richer from the globalization-fuelled growth of the 1990s, and the living standards of most people continued to rise. At the same time, a growing number of people in these countries were losing their jobs as the corporations moved their operations abroad in search of cheaper labour – from Japan to the Philippines, for example. The gap between winners and losers in the rich countries grew wider.

The richer countries were also facing competition from newly developing countries like the **Asian Tigers** and China, which spent far less on providing their peoples with health and welfare benefits. In order to compete successfully with these new rivals, the richer countries had to cut back the **benefits** they paid out to their own peoples. The poorest got less help than before, which also increased inequality.

The rise of international corporations and banks which held such enormous power also posed a threat to national governments. They could no longer feel in complete control of their own countries. This is what one French government discovered in the early 1980s, when it tried to introduce a socialist programme. International business began withdrawing capital from France, which reduced the value of the French currency. The government was forced to reconsider its programme.

Keeping down costs

In Bob Dylan's song 'North Country Blues' (1963), he tells the story of how a North American mine has been forced to close by foreign competition. The South American mine is more competitive because the local workers are prepared to work almost for nothing.

That government, like most in the richer countries, was freely elected by its people. And yet its wishes were simply overridden by the interests of an international business community which no one had elected. As an increasing number of experts were pointing out, globalization clearly had serious consequences for **democracy**.

Consequences for the poorer countries

If the governments of the rich countries could be frightened by the new powers of the international economy, then what hope did the governments of the poor countries have? Their bargaining power was weaker than ever, and they found themselves forced to offer greater and greater incentives (rewards) to the international companies to set up on their home turf. Health and safety regulations were ignored, **tax incentives** and other bribes offered, protesters quickly jailed. As a result, many new factories in the poor countries were strikingly similar to those of early Victorian England, full of very young employees working long hours for very low pay.

This was capitalism's dark side at the beginning of the 21st century. In factories scattered around the poorest countries, young girls spent fourteen-hour work days making famous brand name goods for the sort of wages which only just covered their food and board in an upstairs dormitory. The trainers and clothes they made were then sold on by the local company to brand name companies in the West. These companies then spent more on advertising their brand names than they had on the actual goods, and reaped enormous profits in return.

Consequences for everyone

Globalization has other results for the world as a whole. One is a greater homogeneity, or sameness, in the products which are bought and sold around the world. More and more, you find the same fast foods, clothes brands, music and fashions in the farthest corners of the globe.

The women in this factory in Zhongshan, China are making brand-name trainers for the Western market. They are paid a tiny fraction of the money the trainers will sell for.

The success of Western capitalism at selling Western products may result in uniformity everywhere. There is a serious danger that we will lose much of the world's cultural diversity in the process.

Another consequence is an increasing sense of uncertainty and insecurity. When jobs can be moved so easily from country to country, few jobs are safe. When the world's economies are so interconnected, then bad news for one can easily become bad news for all. An event like the terrorist attack on the World Trade Centre in New York City on 11 September 2001 had economic consequences for almost every family on earth.

The world is becoming increasingly Westernized. McDonald's in Bejing, China looks just like any McDonald's in the USA or Europe.

A brighter outlook?

Capitalism's supporters would argue that for all its problems, and for all its unfairness, capitalism has raised the living standards of almost every community on earth over the last century. Its relentless pursuit of profit continues to create new products, new industries, new ways of looking at the world.

It finds solutions to many of the problems it itself creates – the global Internet, for example, may prove as good for democracy as the power of the multinational corporations has proved dangerous.

New and democratic international political groupings may arise to challenge the undemocratic powers of the world economy. The rise of protests against famous brand names for their exploitation of workers in the poorer countries may persuade corporations, conscious of their image, to change their ways.

Global capitalism is a fairly new development. Like national capitalism in the 19th century, it will need to adapt if it wishes to survive and prosper. And capitalism is nothing if not adaptable.

So, what is capitalism?

Capitalism is an economic system, in which private individuals (or groups) use private **capital** (money or other forms of wealth, like machinery) and labour to produce goods and services. These can be sold at a **profit** in a competitive market which is free and open to everyone. As a form of economic transaction, capitalism goes back a thousand years and more. As the dominant force in any society, it goes back only as far as 18th-century Britain. During that century and the next, it slowly tightened its hold on the economies of western Europe and North America, and over the last hundred years it has effectively conquered the globe.

Until the late 1980s, the Pudong district of Shanghai, China was mostly farmland. Today it has been transformed into a stunning new city, thanks to the capitalist growth machine.

History and politics

The central fact of capitalism is that, left to itself, it tends to generate both wealth and inequality. Everyone on earth has benefited, at least to some degree, from the generation of wealth, but the generation of inequality at the same time has led to many social and political crises.

52

The history of capitalism is an endless search for compromise, between setting it free to make wealth and holding it back with government regulations and restrictions. Without such government intervention, those who work for pay, supplying the labour which turns capital into goods and services, have usually been given an unsatisfactory share of the wealth which they have done most to create.

This was particularly obvious during the **Great Depression**. Afterwards, government intervention in the capitalist economies was at its height. The opposite occurred in the 1970s, 80s and 90s. It was then considered that government intervention had gone too far, and had become a brake on growth. Restrictions were lifted, economies deregulated, and capitalism let off the leash once more.

Generally speaking, it has been governments of the **left** which have favoured intervention, governments of the **right** which have taken their feet off the brakes, but a capitalist system can operate under any government which allows economic freedom to flourish. It is harder to make this work in a situation where there is no political freedom, but it is quite possible. This has been shown by many military governments over the last few decades. Capitalism tends to favour political freedom, but it can do without it.

The only serious attempt to abolish capitalism – to rip it up by the roots – took place in Soviet Russia and those **communist** states like China which followed its example. Some of capitalism's faults were dealt with – guaranteeing every citizen a job, for example, banished the fear of unemployment – but overall the communist experiment was a terrible failure. The replacement of private property and the free market with government planning lessened economic efficiency and took away people's freedom.

53

Protests and prospects

Communism's collapse at the end of the 1980s left capitalism triumphant, but there was little time to enjoy the applause. The gap between rich and poor was widening. Major environmental issues needed attention. Globalization was not only making these problems worse, but also creating new ones for democracy in the richer countries. Through the 1990s, a campaign of protest gathered momentum, as people, angered by exploitation in the poorer countries, or worried about threats to democracy and the environment, came together in a loose alliance against capitalism.

Many believe that all these issues have a common thread – capitalism's basic heartlessness. They feel, in the words of one famous phrase, that capitalism 'knows the price of everything and the real value of nothing'. Most accept that capitalism remains the most efficient generator of wealth, but they point out that the system itself has no interest in helping the less fortunate. Individual capitalists may have such an interest, but it is the desire for profits, and not the desire to help others, which drives the growth machine forward.

Protesters clash with police in Genoa, Italy during a summit meeting of the world's richest nations in 2001.

Since capitalism cannot supply its own conscience, society must provide one for it. Religion used to supply such a conscience, but it is now a much weaker force in the richer countries than it used to be. **Socialism** has tried to supply something similar, pushing for more equality as capitalism pushes for less, but socialism has been tarnished by the disgraceful record of its more extreme cousin, communism. It remains to be seen where competitive, individualistic capitalism will find the conscience it will need in the 21st century.

Contrasting views on capitalism

Capitalism has always provoked controversy and strong opinions. Sylvia Pankhurst, the British campaigner for women's votes, vowed to 'fight capitalism even if it kills me'. She felt it was wrong that 'some people should be comfortable and well-fed while others are starving'. By contrast, the British Prime Minister Winston Churchill remarked that only socialists thought it was wrong to make a profit – the real crime was to make a loss.

In the USA, President Eisenhower spoke admiringly of 'the creative magic of free labour and capital', but his fellow American, the African-American leader Malcolm X, was not convinced. 'Show me a capitalist,' he said, 'I'll show you a bloodsucker.'

Timeline

1492	Columbus discovers the Americas
1500–1800	Age of commercial capitalism
early 1500s	Birth of **Protestantism**
mid-1700s	Beginning of **Industrial Revolution** in UK
1764	James Hargreaves invents spinning-jenny textile machine
1767	Richard Arkwright invents water frame textile machine. Adam Smith's *An Inquiry into the Nature and Causes of the Wealth of Nations* is published
1832	Reform Act increases the number of those allowed to vote in UK
1833	First Factory Act to regulate working conditions is introduced in UK
1848	Karl Marx and Friedrich Engels's *Communist Manifesto* is published
1851	The Great Exhibition is held in London
1860s	Worldwide growth of **socialist** parties
1867	First volume of Karl Marx's *Capital* (*Das Kapital*) published
1870–1914	United States and Germany overtake UK in industrial production
1890	Introduction of **anti-trust laws** in USA (Sherman Act)
1908	Introduction of Ford Model T, the first mass-produced car
1914–18	World War I
1917	The first **communist** revolution takes place in Russia
1918–19	Treaty of Versailles agreed in Paris
1928	Soviet leadership introduces overall economy planning
1929	**Great Crash** on New York Stock Exchange (October)
1929–33	The worst years of the **Great Depression**
1933	President F. D. Roosevelt introduces first New Deal measures
1936	J. M. Keynes's *General Theory of Unemployment, Interest and Money* published
1939–45	World War II
1945	World Bank and International Monetary Fund (IMF) set up

1947	**Cold War** begins. UK gives independence to India (beginning of European decolonization)
1948	General Agreement on Tariffs and Trade (GATT) formed
1949	Founding of the Chinese People's Republic
1950–75	Capitalist economies boom in North America, western Europe and Japan
1957	European Economic Community (EEC) founded
1959	Cuban revolution
1961	Julius Nyerere becomes leader of Tanganyika (later renamed Tanzania)
1963–75	US involvement in Vietnam War
1968	Spring of anti-capitalist protests in France
1973	Sharp rise in price of oil helps to slow down capitalist economies
1974	Friedrich von Hayek wins Nobel Prize for Economics
1976	Milton Friedman wins Nobel Prize for Economics
1978	Deng Xiaoping introduces market reforms in communist China
1979–90	Margaret Thatcher is Prime Minister of UK
1981–89	Ronald Reagan is President of USA
1989–91	The end of **communism** in Europe
1992	European Economic Community (EEC) becomes European Union (EU)
1993	USA, Canada and Mexico form North American Free Trade Area (NAFTA)
1995	World Trade Organization (WTO) is set up as successor to GATT
1997	Kyoto Agreement to control emissions which cause global warming. Economic slowdown begins in **Asian Tiger** economies
1999	Major anti-capitalist protest in Seattle, USA
2001	Terrorist attack on New York and Washington
2002	Protests outside meeting of finance ministers at World Bank-IMF in Washington DC

Further reading

Charles Dickens, *Hard Times* (Penguin, 1994)

David Downing, *The Great Depression* (Heinemann Library, 2001)

R.G. Grant, *Capitalism* (Hodder Wayland, 2000)

John Steinbeck, *The Grapes of Wrath* (Penguin, 1976)

David Taylor, *The Cold War* (Heinemann Library, 2001)

Robert Westall, 'Sea Coal', *The Haunting of Chas McGill* (Macmillan, 1983)

Sources

Peter Donaldson and Harold Pollins, *Capitalism* (Hamish Hamilton, 1978)

Noreena Hertz, *The Silent Takeover* (William Heinemann, 2001)

Naomi Klein, *No Logo* (Flamingo, 2000)

Peter Saunders, *Capitalism, A Social Audit* (Open University Press, 1995)

Adam Smith, *The Wealth of Nations* (Oxford University Press, 1963)

Websites

www.bankofengland.co.uk/

news.ft.com/home/uk

www.imf.org

www.wto.org

www.eco-schools.org.uk

www.yourturn.net

Key figures in the history of capitalism

Henry Ford (1863–1947) was the American engineer who founded the Ford Motor Company in Detroit in 1899. Nine years later he was the first manufacturer to introduce assembly-line production, for his famous Model T.

Milton Friedman (1912–) was the Professor of Economic Science at Chicago University from 1946 to 1983. He championed the **free market**, saying that government intervention in the economy should only be allowed to control **inflation** by limiting the amount of money in circulation. Like von Hayek, he found his ideas growing in popularity after the economic crises of the 1970s. Friedman won the Nobel Prize for Economics in 1976. He served as a policy adviser during Ronald Reagan's two terms as US President (1981–89).

Friedrich von Hayek (1899–1992), influential Austrian economist and political scientist. He held important academic posts in London (1931–50) and Chicago (1950–62). In his most famous book, *The Road to Serfdom* (1944), he defended **liberalism** and the free market capitalism at a time when government intervention in the economy (Keynesianism) was more popular. After the crisis of the capitalist economies in the mid-1970s, many turned to his ideas, and in 1974 he shared the Nobel Prize for Economics.

John Maynard Keynes (1883–1946) was a UK economist who served as an adviser to the government in both World Wars. He criticized the Treaty of Versailles, correctly predicting that the decision to make Germany pay **reparations** would be disastrous for the whole international economy. Throughout the 1920s and 1930s, he argued for increased government intervention to spur economies on and reduce unemployment. His ideas helped to influence President Roosevelt to introduce the New Deal in America.

Vladimir Ilyich Lenin (1870–1924) was the leader of the first **communist** revolution, the second Russian Revolution of 1917. Once in power he took the first steps in the abolition of capitalism in what became the Soviet Union. He vastly reduced private property rights and the operations of a free market.

Karl Marx (1818–83) was the German **philosopher**, economist and political scientist whose theories of social development helped to inspire both **socialism** and communism. His most important work was *Capital (Das Kapital)*, which both examined capitalism in detail and predicted its inevitable downfall.

Ronald Reagan (1911–) was a Hollywood actor who turned to politics. First he became Governor of California and then US President (1981–89). He pursued **right-wing** policies, cutting taxes (particularly on business and the rich) and reducing government spending on provision of **welfare benefits**.

Franklin Delano Roosevelt (1882–1945) was elected President of the USA at the height of the **Great Depression**. His administration introduced the New Deal, a series of policies which involved spending government money to boost the economy and get people back to work.

Adam Smith (1723–90), a Scottish economist and philosopher, is considered by many to be the founder of modern economics. He was the first to champion the emerging system of free market capitalism, and his book, *An Inquiry into the Nature and Causes of the Wealth of Nations* (1876), is still important.

Margaret Thatcher (1925–) took over as leader of the UK Conservative Party in 1975, and four years later became the first UK woman Prime Minister (1979–90). Her government, the most right-wing the UK had seen in 50 years, championed free market capitalism and tried to reduce government intervention in the economy. The power of the **trade unions** was lessened, and publicly owned industries were returned to private ownership.

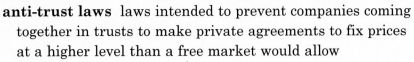

Glossary

anti-trust laws laws intended to prevent companies coming together in trusts to make private agreements to fix prices at a higher level than a free market would allow

aristocracy those who have inherited membership of the ruling elite by birth

Asian Tigers countries in the Far East and Southeast Asia which experienced rapid economic growth in the late 1990s

benefits payment made by government to those who, for various reasons, are unable to work

capital money or other forms of wealth (such as land or machinery) which can be used to create goods or services

Cold War name given to the hostility that existed between the free enterprise capitalist and communist worlds between 1947 and the late 1980s

colonialism rule of economically undeveloped countries by economically advanced countries.

communism originally an extreme form of socialism, in which property is owned communally (in common) rather than individually. The term 'communism' later became associated with the dictatorial state and system of economic planning which was created in the Soviet Union during the 1920s and 30s.

democracy political system in which governments are regularly elected by the mass of the people, or a country in which this system exists

democratic reflecting the wishes of all those involved, often through voting

dictatorship government by an individual or a small group in which the mass of people have no say

Enlightenment period of the 18th century in which many European philosophers put more importance on reason and individualism than on tradition

exploitation taking advantage of, using selfishly or unfairly

fascism dictatorial system of government originating in Italy, which was later known for its aggressive nationalism. Nazism was one type of fascism.

fixed capital capital used to turn working capital into products; for example, the machinery used to make goods

five-year plan in communist countries, a plan of all intended economic activity over a five-year period

free market market which government does not regulate, or only regulates a little

global warming the gradual warming of the Earth's atmosphere, which is mostly caused by rising levels of carbon dioxide gas

Great Crash sudden collapse of share values on the New York Stock Exchange in October 1929, which helped to trigger the Great Depression

Great Depression period of great economic hardship that began around 1929, peaked around 1933, and lasted for most of the following decade. Most countries of the world were affected

Industrial Revolution the change from a primarily agricultural economy to one based on large-scale production in factories which began in England in the 18th century

inflation increase in prices or increase in the supply of money (which leads to an increase in prices)

interest payments money repaid at regular intervals on a loan

interest rates when a loan is repaid, the extra amount charged for being allowed to take the loan

investment putting money into a project, in the hope of making a profit

left(-wing) in politics, usually associated with policies which place the needs of the whole community (everyone) above the short-term wants of the individual

liberalism in the 19th century, a belief in the free market, free trade, and the removal of obstacles to either

multinational corporation large business which operates in several countries

philosopher someone who thinks, and often writes, about the bigger questions of human life

privatization returning publicly owned companies to private ownership

profit the difference between what is paid out and what comes back, when the latter is more than the former. For example, if an orange is bought for ten pence (or cents) and sold for fifteen, then the seller makes a profit of five pence ($15 - 10 = 5$).